I0804647

Disability PRIDE

Language Matters

Jill Keppeler

PowerKiDS press

Published in 2025 by The Rosen Publishing Group, Inc.
2544 Clinton Street, Buffalo, NY 14224

Copyright © 2025 by The Rosen Publishing Group, Inc.

All rights reserved. No part of this book may be reproduced in any form without permission in writing from the publisher, except by a reviewer.

Editor: Michele Suchomel-Casey
Book Design: Leslie Taylor

Photo Credits: Cover wavebreakmedia/Shutterstock.com; (series background) P.siripak/Shutterstock.com, (series disability pride colors) rudall30/Shutterstock.com; p. 5 WBMUL/Shutterstock.com, (flag sidebar) Maxim Studio/Shutterstock.com; p. 7 Kit Leong/Shutterstock.com; p. 9 Lopolo/Shutterstock.com; p. 10 Monkey Business Images/Shutterstock.com; p. 11 wavebreakmedia/Shutterstock.com; p. 13 Rawpixel.com/Shutterstock.com; p. 15 Denis Kuvaev/Shutterstock.com; p. 17 Ground Picture/Shutterstock.com; p. 19 SynthEx/Shutterstock.com; p. 21 GagliardiPhotography/Shutterstock.com.

Cataloging-in-Publication Data

Names: Keppeler, Jill.
Title: Language matters / Jill Keppeler.
Description: Buffalo, NY : PowerKids Press, 2025. | Series: Disability pride | Includes glossary and index.
Identifiers: ISBN 9781499446838 (pbk.) | ISBN 9781499446845 (library bound) | ISBN 9781499446852 (ebook)
Subjects: LCSH: People with disabilities–Juvenile literature. | People with disabilities–Social conditions–Juvenile literature. | People with disabilities–Civil rights–Juvenile literature.
Classification: LCC HV1568.K54 2025 | DDC 362.4–dc23

Manufactured in the United States of America

Some of the images in this book illustrate individuals who are models. The depictions do not imply actual situations or events.

CPSIA Compliance Information: Batch #CSPK25. For Further Information contact Rosen Publishing at 1-800-237-9932.

Find us on

Contents

We're All Different

Everyone in the world is different. We look different, we speak in different ways, and we like different things. We also all have different abilities. There are things we can do well and things that perhaps we don't do as well. Many people have disabilities, or conditions that limit or change what they can do or the way they can do it.

People may have disabilities that affect their senses or movement. There are disabilities that affect how people think and learn. Sometimes, these disabilities are visible, and sometimes they're not. There are many ways in which we're all different!

Sometimes people with disabilities have useful tools to help them, such as a wheelchair.

The disability pride flag was created to show acceptance and respect for people who have disabilities. Each color is for a different type of disability.

- The gray background is in honor of those who've died.
- Green is for disabilities that have to do with the senses.
- Blue is for those that have to with the mind and emotions.
- White stands for unseen disabilities, as well as those that haven't been diagnosed, or found out.
- Gold is for neurodiversity.
- Red is for other disabilities of the body.

The Disability Rights Movement

Once, many people didn't think that those with disabilities had an equal right to things other people had, like **access** to jobs, housing, and other basic human rights. This often included the right to have basic respect, including with the words used to talk about disability.

Around the middle of the 20th century, people with disabilities and their supporters started working together to demand more rights. This has been a long fight, but over time, the government has passed laws about disability rights. People also have learned more about the words used to talk about disability.

People are still fighting for disability rights. This photo shows people at the 2022 Disability Rights Are Human Rights event in front of the U.S. Capitol building in Washington, D.C.

Learn More

The Americans with Disabilities Act (ADA) was signed into law in 1990. This law makes it illegal to **discriminate** against people because of disabilities.

Changing Language

People used to use language that was dehumanizing to refer to those with disabilities. This means that the words made it sound like those with disabilities weren't real people with feelings and dreams and goals like everyone else. Often the people using this language weren't trying to be mean. (Though sometimes they were.) Those were just the words used back then.

This doesn't mean using this language is right today. It's important to change the language we use as we learn more about it, the world around us, and how it makes people feel.

Learn More

Some people use outdated words about disability to call others mean names. The Spread the Word campaign (spreadtheword.global) aims to end this form of **exclusion**.

While some words used to refer to disabilities can i
be mean, some have good **intentions** behin
But good intentions don't mean th
just
them.

A Part of Life

It's clearly important to avoid using mean names about people with disabilities. No one likes that! But sometimes it's also key to simply stop and think about whether you need to mention a disability (that isn't yours) at all. Does it have anything to do with what you're talking about? No? Then why bring it up?

That doesn't mean it's not OK to talk about disabilities. They're part of life! If someone with a disability is OK talking about it and you're curious, just be polite and take your cues from them. Treat others [illegible] you'd like to [illegible]ted.

We all have differences, and it can be good to learn about them! Different abilities also means different strengths.

Ask and Listen

One very important rule when talking about disabilities is simply to ask—and then to listen. What one person prefers may not be what another person prefers. Some people dislike certain words and terms about their disability. Others may prefer them. As long as you're not using mean or outdated words, use what they prefer.

There's not a one-size-fits-all answer to questions about the language around disabilities. Again, everyone is different. There are differences between people with different disabilities and between people with the same disabilities. Everyone in a group doesn't have to be the same—and probably isn't!

You might want to help someone you
know with a disability. But it's ver
important to always ask fir
they don't want o

Person First?

Many people with disabilities prefer what's called "person-first" language. This is language that avoids **defining** people in terms of their disability. It often means putting the reference to a person before the reference to the disability. For example, this means saying things like, "a person with Down syndrome," "a person with autism," "a person with hearing loss," etc.

However, some people don't like person-first language for themselves. They may think it suggests that their disability is **negative**, when they feel that it's a key part of their **identity**. This is one reason it's important to ask what people prefer if you need to refer to them and their disability.

More

It's still best to use person-first language if you need to refer to people and disabilities in general—or specifically, if you don't know what they prefer.

Down syndrome is a condition in which a
person may have **developmental** delays
or other **traits**, but not all people with
Down syndrome are the same.

No "Normal"

Sometimes the words we use to refer to people without disabilities are just as important. "Normal" seems like a fairly harmless word. It means "usual," "regular," or "fitting to type." But who's to say what's normal? What's normal for one person isn't what's normal for others. Don't use "normal" or words like it to refer to those without disabilities. After all, if a person has Down syndrome, that's normal for them.

Also avoid saying things that make those with disabilities seem as if they're passive, or not taking an active part in their own lives. This includes calling people "victims" of their disability or saying that they "suffer" from something.

Just because someone has a disability doesn't mean there's something wrong with them! We all have our own differences.

Learn More

In a similar way, be careful with words about h
and disability. People can have disabi
chronic condition and still be heal
not an illness!

Mental Health

Language around mental health and related disabilities is important too. There are a lot of commonly used words that can spread stereotypes about people with these disabilities. It can be really easy to accidentally use one of these words in a way that isn't meant to be mean but still spreads the wrong ideas.

That includes words like "crazy" or "nuts." In the past, these words were used for people with mental health issues, but many people are trying to learn to use better language. There's a **stigma** to being treated for these issues that keeps people from getting help, and changing our language is one big way to fight that stigma.

A stereotype is a commonly held idea about a group of people that isn't based in reality. One common stereotype about mental health issues is that they can make people unsafe.

Learn More

Kids can have mental health issues too. They can affect how you deal with feelings and how you pay attention in school. It's important to talk to a trusted adult if you think you might need help.

Words Have Power

Some people say that words can't hurt you, but that's not true. Words can hurt a lot! However, they can also strengthen people and help give them power. This includes the power to choose the words they themselves prefer and to ask others to use those words. It's all about respect and listening to others.

People with disabilities aren't just one big group in which every person is the same. That's why it's so important to speak and to listen to individuals with disabilities. The world will keep changing, and people will keep learning more. Language will continue to change, and we can change with it!

Language and words can hurt, but they can help bring us together too.

Glossary

access: The ability to use or enter something.

chronic: Continuing or occurring again and again.

define: To determine the qualities or meaning of something.

developmental: Related to growing and changing.

discriminate: To treat people unequally based on class, race, or religion.

exclusion: The state of being excluded, or kept out of something.

identity: The qualities, beliefs, etc., that make a particular person or group different from others.

intention: An aim or plan.

negative: Considered harmful, bad, or unwanted.

stigma: A set of negative, often unfair beliefs that a society or group of people have about something.

trait: A quality that makes one person or thing different from another.

For More Information

BOOKS

Hoffman, Alexandra. *Masterpiece*. Edmonton, Alberta, Canada: Wishing Star Press, 2022.

Shodja, Vona B. *Zee Zee Does It Anyway!* Lioness Cove Publishing, 2022.

Webb, Amy. *Awesomely Emma*. Minneapolis, MN: Beaming Books, 2022.

WEBSITES

The Fight for Disability Rights
junior.scholastic.com/pages/promotion/031521/the-fight-for-disability-rights.html
Junior Scholastic presents a look at the path of disability rights in the United States.

Spread the Word: Inclusion
www.spreadtheword.global/
This campaign to end the use of an excluding word about disability has expanded to promote all forms of inclusion.

Publisher's note to educators and parents: Our editors have carefully reviewed these websites to ensure that they are suitable for students. Many websites change frequently, however, and we cannot guarantee that a site's future contents will continue to meet our high standards of quality and educational value. Be advised that students should be closely supervised whenever they access the internet.

Index